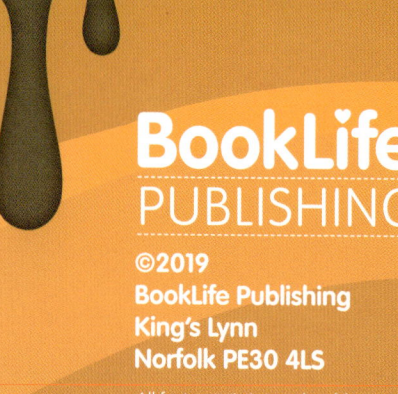

©2019
BookLife Publishing
King's Lynn
Norfolk PE30 4LS

All rights reserved.
Printed in Malaysia.

A catalogue record for this book is available from the British Library.

ISBN: 978-1-78637-514-8

Written by:
Holly Duhig

Edited by:
Kirsty Holmes

Designed by:
Jasmine Pointer

All facts, statistics, web addresses and URLs in this book were verified as valid and accurate at time of writing. No responsibility for any changes to external websites or references can be accepted by either the author or publisher.

Photocredits:
Images are courtesy of Shutterstock.com. With thanks to Getty Images, Thinkstock Photo and iStockphoto.

Frederik the Fly: Natthapon Boochagorn & Roi and Roi. Front cover - Sunflowerr, Memo Angeles, MaryValery, Creative Mood, Macrovector, Useless_Graphic, Maquiladora. 5 - Eric Isselee, Nathapol Kongseang, LiskaM, photolinc, StockSmartStart, PiXXart. 6 - Top Vector Studio, jenykorney. 7 - pathdoc, Anastasiia Kucherenko. 8 - Paul Reeves Photography. 9 - Atovot. 10 - MartinMaritz. 11 - Jan Mastnik. 12 - Karel Cerny. 13 – pikepicture. 14 - Tao Jiang. 15 - Eric Isselee. 16 - Iconic Bestiary, Javier Brosch. 18 - Cheryl E. Davis. 19 - Sara Robinson. 20 - Kirill Dorofeev. 21 - COMMON THINGS. 22 - StudioSmart. 23 - Macrovector, Daniel Prudek.

Contents

PAGE 4   Animals Eat What?!
PAGE 6   Plates of Poo
PAGE 8   Ravenous Rabbits
PAGE 10   Dung Diners
PAGE 12   Poopy Pandas
PAGE 14   Cheeky Chimps
PAGE 16   Puppy Puke
PAGE 18   Bird Barf
PAGE 20   Mouth to Mouth
PAGE 22   Do You Eat Sick?
PAGE 24   Glossary and Index

WORDS THAT LOOK LIKE **THIS** CAN BE FOUND IN THE GLOSSARY ON PAGE 24.

Animals Eat What?!

All animals, including humans, need to eat food to stay alive. However, some animals have different ideas about what counts as 'food'…

IT IS I, FREDERICK THE FLY, WORLD-FAMOUS CRITIC OF UNUSUAL FOOD!

Plates of Poo

As a human you'd probably never dream of tucking into a plate of sick or a big pile of dog poo but, for many animals, these disgusting dinners are what keep them alive and healthy!

LOTS OF ANIMALS RELY ON THEIR OWN OR OTHER ANIMAL'S POO FOR IMPORTANT NUTRIENTS.

Eating poo is called coprophagia (cop-ro-FAY-jee-ah).
You might be thinking, "That's gross!" This is probably a good thing. Scientists believe humans <u>evolved</u> to be disgusted by poo and sick because these smelly bodily functions can carry some pretty harmful diseases.

⚠️ IF YOU'RE A HUMAN READING THIS, NEVER EAT POO – OR SICK FOR THAT MATTER. IT WILL MAKE YOU VERY ILL!

Ravenous Rabbits

Rabbits mostly eat plants and weeds. Grass is high in <u>fibre</u> which is hard to <u>digest</u> so – by the time their food has made it all the way to the other end – it still has lots of juicy nutrients!

Rabbits can tell which of their droppings are safe to eat again by their colour. The softer, black droppings are called cecotropes (see-ko-tropes) and are the most nutritious. Rabbits will eat these straight from their bum!

RABBITS DON'T LET ALL THE NUTRIENTS IN THEIR POO GO TO, WELL... WASTE! RAISINS ANYONE?

PRESENTATION:
 10

TASTE:
 4

SMELL:
 1

TEXTURE:
 4

TOTAL SCORE: 19

Dung Diners

TO ME.

TO YOU.

Perhaps one of the most famous poo-eaters of the animal kingdom is the dung beetle. Dung beetles like to eat the poo of animals such as kangaroos. They are also famous for rolling the poo they find into balls. But where are they going with all that poo?

Sometimes they bury the poo and save it for later. At other times, female dung beetles will lay their eggs in it. When the eggs hatch, the <u>larvae</u> have plenty of dung to feed on.

DUNG BEETLE LARVA

PRESENTATION: 10

TASTE: 6

SMELL: 5

TEXTURE: 5

TOTAL SCORE: 26

YOU HUMANS MIGHT PREFER DOUGH BALLS, BUT HAVE YOU GIVEN DUNG BALLS A FAIR TRY? DON'T KNOCK IT 'TILL YOU TRY IT!

Poopy Pandas

ADULT PANDAS POO AROUND 40 TIMES A DAY!

You thought these fluffy, black-and-white bears were cute didn't you? Well think again. These cute little cubs will happily munch on poo. And not just any poo – their own mother's poo!

Scientists think panda cubs do this because their mother's poo has lots of good <u>bacteria</u>. For lots of animals, including humans, having lots of good bacteria in their gut helps them to digest food.

PRESENTATION: 1
TASTE: 9
SMELL: 9
TEXTURE: 5
TOTAL SCORE: 24

ADULT PANDAS MOSTLY JUST EAT BAMBOO WHICH DOESN'T HAVE A LOT OF NUTRIENTS.

"THIS IS DELICIOUS, BUT NOT VERY NUTRITIOUS!"

Love, Mum xx

Cheeky Chimps

THESE WATERMELON SEEDS WILL BE JUST AS GOOD THE SECOND TIME ROUND!

Chimpanzees aren't known for their table manners, and many are guilty of tucking into their own poo. This is thought to be because their poo still has seeds in it that haven't been properly digested.

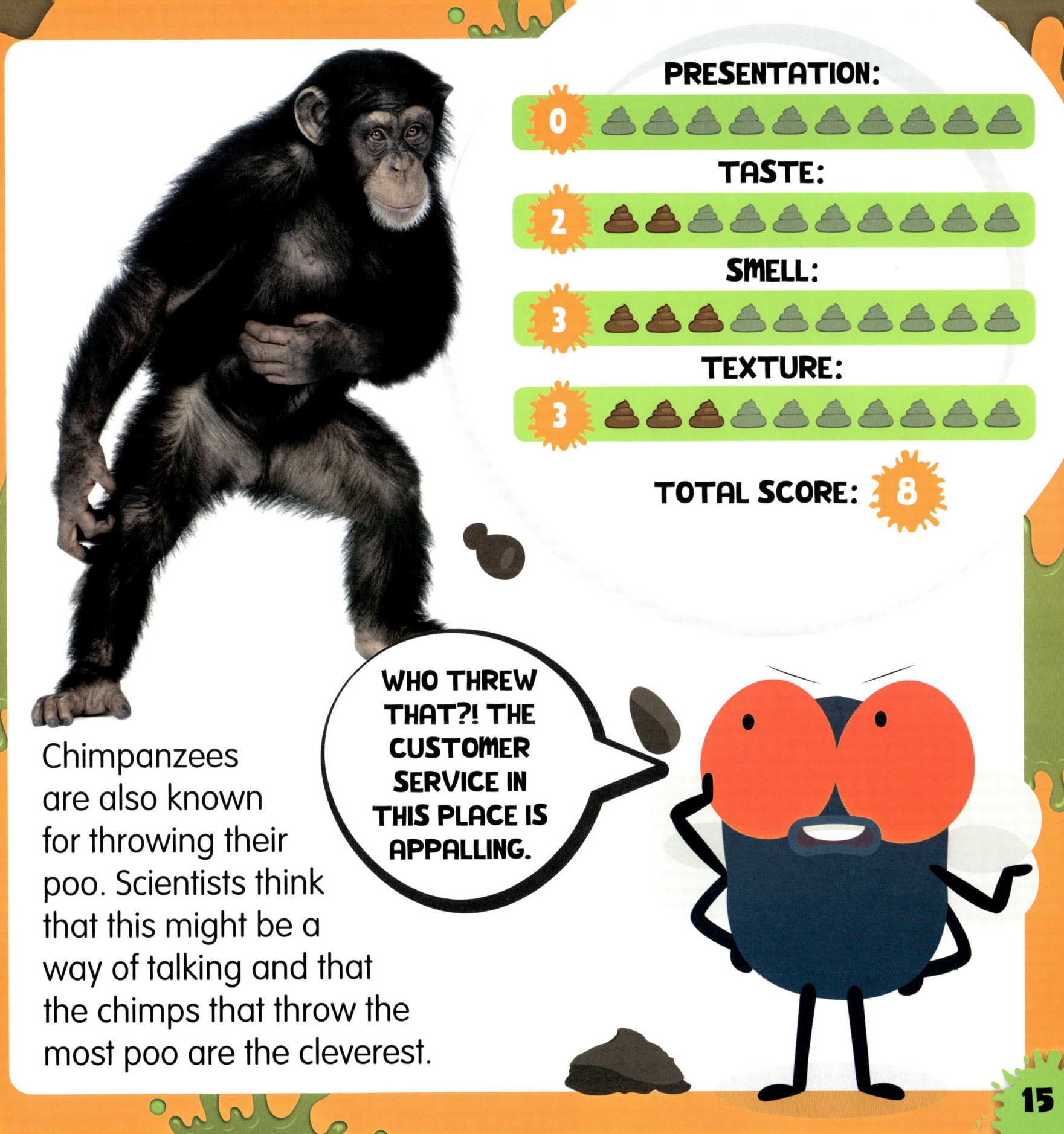

PRESENTATION: 0

TASTE: 2

SMELL: 3

TEXTURE: 3

TOTAL SCORE: 8

WHO THREW THAT?! THE CUSTOMER SERVICE IN THIS PLACE IS APPALLING.

Chimpanzees are also known for throwing their poo. Scientists think that this might be a way of talking and that the chimps that throw the most poo are the cleverest.

Puppy Puke

Have you ever had a sickness bug that left you puking up your guts? If so, hopefully the last thing that crossed your mind after being sick was gobbling it all back up again. For dogs, it's a different story.

Dogs have a very good sense of smell. A dog's sense of smell is around 40 times better than a human's. When they smell their own sick, they smell all the little bits of food going to waste.

Bird Barf

Whatever your parents make you for dinner tonight it will never be as bad as what bird parents feed their children. Mother birds will leave the nest, swallow a juicy worm or two and then...

They will <u>regurgitate</u> this tasty snack into the mouths of their babies.

Doing this means that birds can carry more food to their babies. After all, there's more space in their stomachs than in their beaks.

FINALLY. A MEAL I'VE NEVER TRIED BEFORE! I'M NOT SURE THAT HALF-DIGESTED WORMS ARE MY FAVOURITE DISH, BUT WE'LL SOON FIND OUT.

PRESENTATION:
 0

TASTE:
 5

SMELL:
 5

TEXTURE:
 7

TOTAL SCORE:  17

Mouth to Mouth

BUT I DON'T WANT TO SHARE!

Like birds, orangutans also feed their babies from their mouths. Orangutan mothers will chew, or <u>masticate</u>, food until it is nice and mushy, and then spit it into their baby's mouth.

The mother's saliva (spit) breaks down the food so that her baby gets more nutrients from it. When they are first born, orangutan babies are fed with their mother's milk. Eating chewed-up food gets them used to eating solid food instead of milk.

PRESENTATION: 1
TASTE: 8
SMELL: 5
TEXTURE: 10
TOTAL SCORE: 24

THE PRESENTATION COULD DO WITH SOME IMPROVEMENT, BUT I'VE ALWAYS LOVED MASHED BANANA!

Do You Eat Sick?

I MADE THIS WITH MY MOUTH!

Bees store the <u>nectar</u> they collect from plants in their honey stomach. When they get back to the hive, they regurgitate the nectar into another bee's mouth.

PRESENTATION:
10 💩💩💩💩💩💩💩💩💩💩

TASTE:
10 💩💩💩💩💩💩💩💩💩💩

SMELL:
10 💩💩💩💩💩💩💩💩💩💩

TEXTURE:
0 💩💩💩💩💩💩💩💩💩💩

TOTAL SCORE: 30

"HONEY IS MY FAVOURITE SICKY DELICACY! ALTHOUGH, IT CAN GET YOU INTO A STICKY SITUATION!"

The bees keep passing on the nectar, mouth to mouth, and chewing it over until it becomes sticky, sweet honey.

Glossary

BACTERIA — microscopic living things that can cause diseases
CRITIC — someone whose job it is to judge something, such as food
DIGEST — to break down food so that it can be used by the body
EVOLVED — gradually developed over a long time
FIBRE — the parts of fruits and vegetables that cannot be digested
LARVAE — a type of young insect that must grow and change before it can reach its adult form
MASTICATE — to chew, crush or grind food
NECTAR — a sweet liquid made by flowers in order to attract insects
NUTRIENTS — natural substances that plants and animals need to grow and stay healthy
REGURGITATE — to vomit food back up into the mouth from the stomach

Index

BACTERIA 13
BEAK 19
DIGEST 8, 13–14, 19
DUNG 10–11
FIBRE 8
GUT 13, 16
LARVAE 11
MASTICATE 20
MOUTH 18, 20, 22–23
NUTRIENTS 6, 8–9, 13, 21
REGURGITATION 18, 22
SALIVA 21
SEEDS 14
STOMACH 19, 22